AMAZING ANIMALS

Fantastic Forest

KINGFISHER
LONDON & NEW YORK

Text copyright © Tony Mitton 2010
Illustrations copyright © Ant Parker 2010
Published in the United States by Kingfisher,
175 Fifth Ave., New York, NY 10010
Kingfisher is an imprint of Macmillan Children's Books, London.
All rights reserved.

Consultancy by David Burnie

Distributed in the U.S. by Macmillan, 175 Fifth Ave., New York, NY 10010
Distributed in Canada by H.B. Fenn and Company Ltd., 34 Nixon Road, Bolton, Ontario L7E 1W2

Library of Congress Cataloging-in-Publication data has been applied for.

ISBN: 978-0-7534-3007-1

Kingfisher books are available for special promotions and premiums. For details contact:
Special Markets Department, Macmillan, 175 Fifth Avenue, New York, NY 10010.

For more information, please visit www.kingfisherbooks.com

Printed in China
1 3 5 7 9 8 6 4 2

To all at The Brunswick Nursery, Cambridge, U.K.
Best wishes, Tony Mitton
For Charlie and Chester—Ant Parker

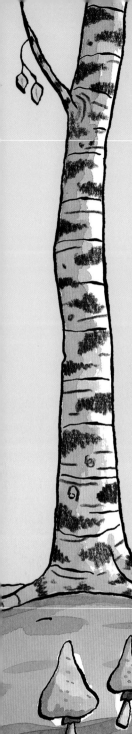

AMAZING ANIMALS
Fantastic Forest

Tony Mitton and Ant Parker

KINGFISHER
NEW YORK

In North American forests,
many trees are evergreen.

And what a lot of creatures live there,
waiting to be seen!

Black bears are good at climbing.
Just see how well they do.

These bears are fetching insects
and pinecone nuts to chew.

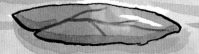

Moose like eating water plants.
Their legs are long and thin.

When it's time for feeding,
they just go wading in.

When skunks are feeling threatened,
they shoot a smelly spray.

The stink's so very strong
it drives most enemies away!

The graceful flying squirrel
can float from tree to tree.

Between its front and back legs
are flaps for gliding, see?

But look, the cougar's prowling.
Keep quiet and stay well clear.

Though strong and fierce,
the cougar's shy and mainly preys on deer.

The porcupine has sharp, barbed quills
that pierce fur or skin.

Most animals can't pull them out,
once they're sticking in!

Chipmunks love to nibble
on a berry, nut, or seed.

They have to sleep through winter
so in summertime they feed.

The long-eared owl has two big tufts of feathers on its head.

At dusk it swoops out hunting
when it's ready to be fed.

Our trip has shown us creatures
in trees and on the ground.

But if we take another look,
which others can be found?

Did you find . . .

the lynx?

the crossbill?

the snowshoe hare?

the osprey?

the marten?

the beaver?

the wolverine?

the spruce
grouse?